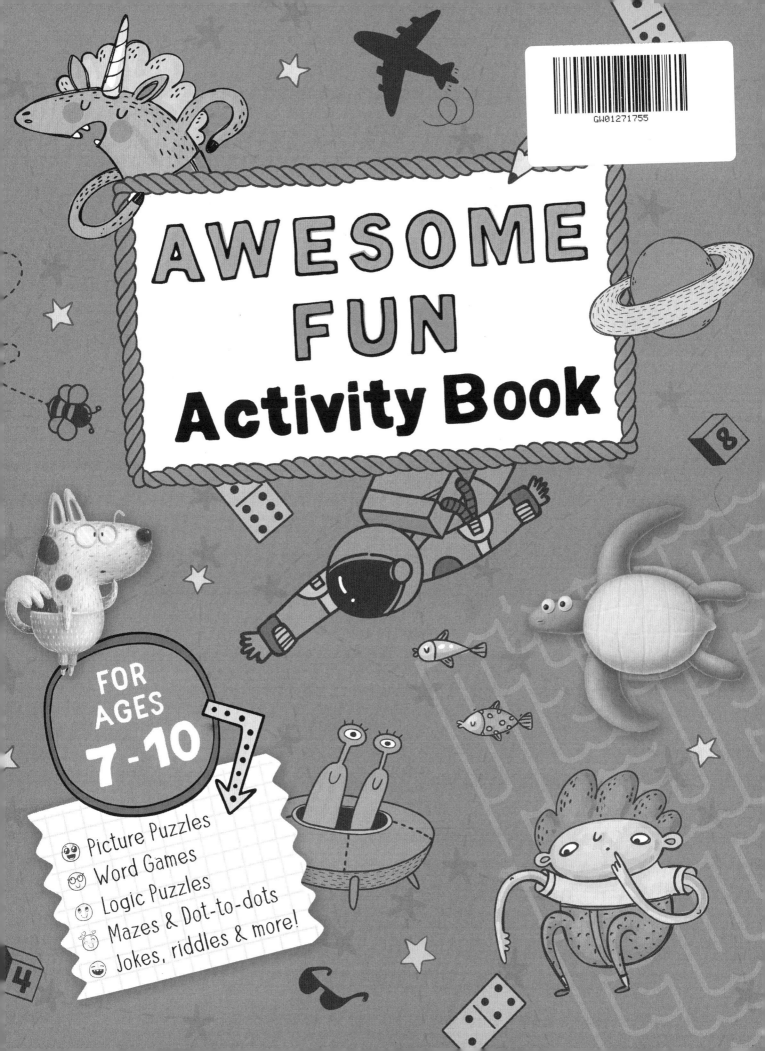

GARDEN ANIMAL CROSSWORD

DOWN

1. A buzzy pollinator
2. A small green jumping animal that lays eggs in ponds
4. A baby butterfly
5. A homing bird that coos
8. A nut collector with a bushy tail
9. A small red beetle with black spots
11. A long-eared cute animal

ACROSS

3. A tree-taping bird
6. An animal with eight legs
7. A beautiful insect with colourful wings
8. A slow creeper that leaves slimy trails
10. A flying insect with a long body and two pairs of strong wings
12. A small rodent that squeaks
13. A common garden bird with black feathers
14. A small spiny mammal that lives in hedges

4 X 4 Sudoku

Put numbers in the empty squares so that every row, column, and box with thicker lines includes the numbers 1, 2, 3, and 4.

A

			1
2		3	4
	2	4	
4	3	1	2

B

		4	
	1	2	3
1			2
2	3	1	

C

			3
	3		
3		1	
	1	3	2

D

2		1	3
	3	2	
4	1		

SPOT THE PAIR

Can you spot which two pictures are exactly the same?

SUMMER WORD SEARCH

Find all of these summer words in the grid below.

SEASIDE	DAISY	POPSICLE
SUNNY	NATURE	LEMONADE
HOLIDAY	SUNFLOWER	SANDALS
PICNIC	CAMPING	POOL
SANDCASTLE	BRIGHT	SEAGULL
OUTDOORS	BUTTERFLIES	ADVENTURE
WARMTH	SUNGLASSES	WATERMELON

```
S S B A A E S R O O D T U O Y S I A D Y
M U G Q J Q H S S E A S I D E J D L K J
M N N S A N D A L S I E L C I S P O P B
H F I E T T E N A T Y X V P X O A Y H F
T L P V A T J D M B U T T E R F L I E S
M O M L S E N C F S C X G M P E N M E T
R W A Y A J J A S N E R T B E O X R V Y
A E C L E Q R S A E D S R F L U U P O A
W R N I E J V T Q J A I S E S T L O I D
W N N F U M D L D C G G M A N F Z G M I
S A A P Z B O E Y H I R U E L Q O Z D L
U T E T O N S N T I E N V L Q G X K V O
N K E Y U O U U A T B D C F L H N J U H
N K V B B R L T A D A N W I G M F U O D
Y S A Q M Z E W T F E Z F O P F Q Y S F
```

Why doesn't the **farmer** know how many **sheep** he

Because he **falls asleep** every time he tries to count them!

What's the difference between a **butterfly** and a **fly**?

A **butterfly** can fly, but a **fly** can't butterfly.

Why does Sunday always win when **arm wrestling** with Monday?

Because Monday is a **weak-day**!

SYMMETRY CHALLENGES

Use the grid to help you complete these symmetrical images!

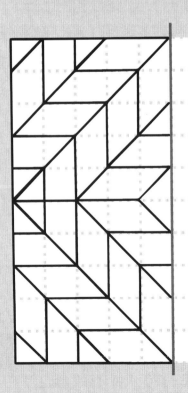

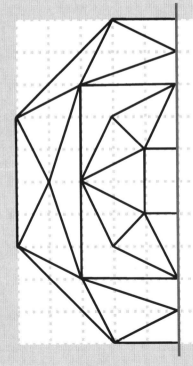

Which House?

Read the clues and help the lost dog find its house.

> My house is next to a tree.
> It doesn't have a flag.
> It has more than one window.
> It doesn't have a fence.
> It doesn't have front door steps.
> It has a round window.

DOT-TO-DOT

Join the dots from 1 to 70 to find out what's under the sea.

DOMINOES

Place the domino pieces on the left in the grey spaces below to complete the domino spiral.

Each domino has two halves, only the halves with the same number can touch each other. For example, this domino has six dots on one half and zero dots on the other, so only dominoes with six dots or zero dots can be placed next to it.

WORD JIGSAW

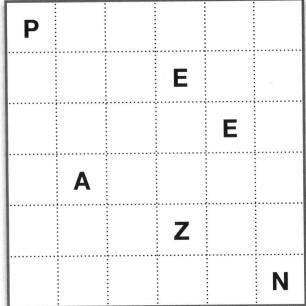

Place the jigsaw pieces below into the grid to complete the puzzle.

The letters spell out six words related to the tropics. The word on the top line is a tropical bird that mimics sounds.

OCEAN CLEAN UP

Find all 15 pieces of plastic waste in the ocean scene so it can be clean up!

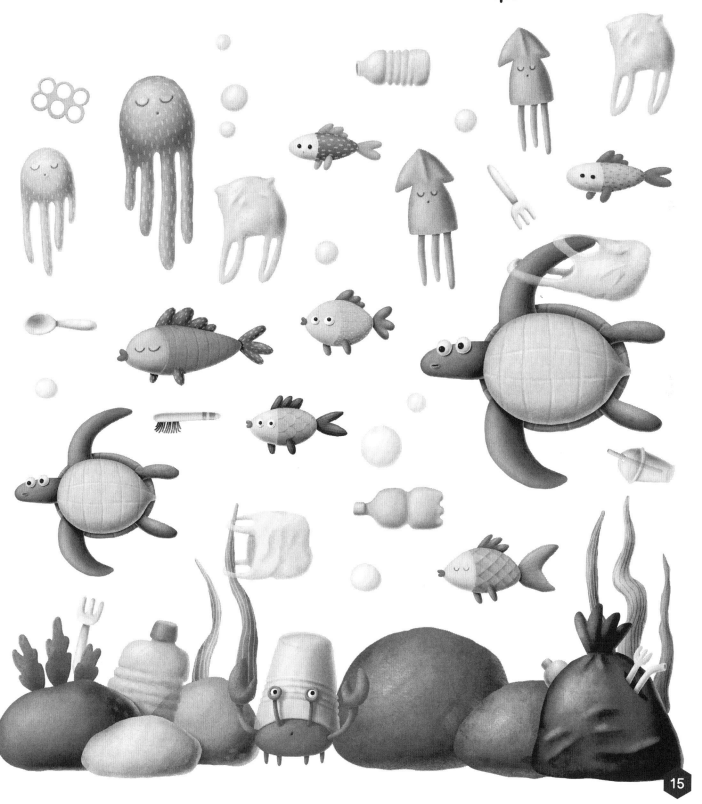

NUMBER PYRAMID

In this pyramid, the number in each square is the sum of the two numbers below it. Can you fill in all the empty squares?

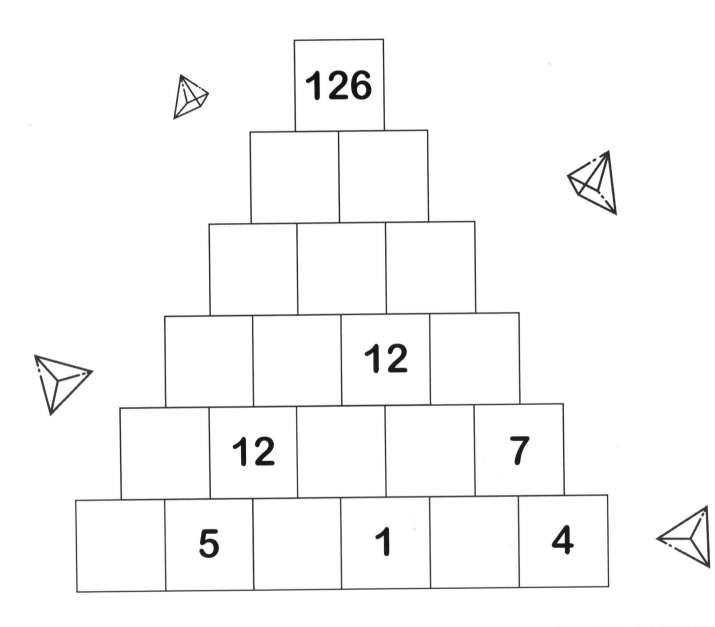

JOKE TIME

What did one **pyramid** say to the other?

How is your __ __ __ __ __ ?

BROKEN WORDS

Can you read the clues below and piece these broken words back together? They are words we use to describe our pets.

CLUES

1. Soft and covered in fluff
2. Making a lot of noise
3. Being impolite in an amusing way
4. Badly behaved
5. Quick to learn, intelligent
6. Amusing and comical
7. Attractive in an endearing way
8. Greatly loved or treasured
9. Pleasant and charming, not bitter or salty
10. Very good looking

CU | EET | TIFUL
IOUS | CLE | FFY
NOI | NAU | NY
FUN | EKY | SW
VER | CHE | SY
GHTY | TE | BEAU
PREC | FLU

1. _ _ _ _ _
2. _ _ _ _ _
3. _ _ _ _ _ _
4. _ _ _ _ _ _ _ _
5. _ _ _ _ _ _ _
6. _ _ _ _ _
7. _ _ _ _
8. _ _ _ _ _ _ _ _
9. _ _ _ _ _
10. _ _ _ _ _ _ _ _ _

4 X 4 Sudoku

Put numbers in the empty squares so that every row, column, and box with thicker lines includes the numbers 1, 2, 3, and 4.

A

			3
4		1	
3		2	
			1

B

	3	2	4
		1	
3			
	2		1

C

	3		
	2	3	1
2		4	3

D

4			3
1		4	
2		3	
			1

18

YOUR OWN COMIC
Create your own superhero and story!

SHADOW WORD GUESS

What animal do the shadows belong to?

Read the highlighted column to find out what is the national animal of Australia

___ _____

MAZE RACE!

You'll need to find someone to do this race with, a friend, a sibling, or a parent. Pick a maze each and start at the same time. The person who gets to the finish first wins!

Follow these step-by-step instructions to learn to draw these yummy treats!

MUSICAL INSTRUMENT WORD SEARCH

Find the instruments hidden in the grid below!

```
N U K U L E L E F B A N J O
A C C O R D I O N G T E V F
Z D P T T E V F D A T Y M W
N I L O I V B X M X N V K Z
C Y F T V A Q B C U A C G H
M E Y F B T O M F L U T E A
J H N U I U R R G O K N G O
G S T O R S Q I T U R Q E Y
P I V I H V M J A E I P R V
I B N W Q P M U D N F T G Y
A E T G Z N O R R H G X A R
N Q R X V C O X U G A L K R
O G U K O C Z E A F Q R E L
M A M F E X K T U S B V P O
H M P R A Z W O N T D N O L
K B E C U U A Y D Z M P H L
U Y T C Z D R U M Q V P C E
O X J T P U S D Y M A Z Q C
```

DRUM
BANJO
HARP
FLUTE
GUITAR
RECORDER
TRUMPET
TRIANGLE
SAXOPHONE
ACCORDION
TAMBOURINE
UKULELE
TUBA
PIANO
VIOLIN
CELLO

23

ARROW WORDS

The clues of this puzzle are in the grey squares, and the arrow from the clue points where the answer word should go. All the words go from left to right, or top to bottom, no matter which direction the arrow points. Some of the clues are pictures!

SPOT THE DIFFERENCE

Find the 10 differences between these two pictures.

SHADOW MATCH

Can you find the correct shadow for these funny monsters?

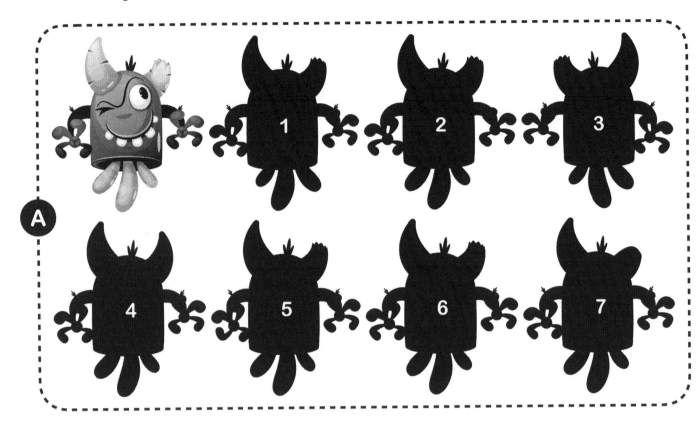

COLOUR BY NUMBERS

1 - BLUE 4 - BROWN
2 - YELLOW 5 - RED
3 - ORANGE 6 - GREEN

I scream, you scream, we all scream for ice cream.

Red lorry, yellow lorry. (Repeat a few times)

She sells seashells on the seashore.
The shells she sells are seashells, I'm sure.
And if she sells seashells on the seashore,
then I'm sure she sells seashore shells.

If two witches were watching two watches, which witch would watch which watch?

The big bug bit the little beetle, but the little beetle bit the big bug back.

TRY THESE TONGUE TWISTERS!

I can think of six thin things, but I can think of six thick things too.

Peter Piper picked a peck of pickled peppers;
A peck of pickled peppers Peter Piper picked;
If Peter Piper picked a peck of pickled peppers,
Where's the peck of pickled peppers Peter Piper picked?

DOT TO DOT

Join the dots from 1 to 70 to uncover the vehicle.

JOKE TIME

Why did the **cow** cross the **road**?

To go to the **moo-vies**!

TRACING LINES

One of the shapes below is impossible to trace without going over a line twice or taking off your pen. Can you find it?

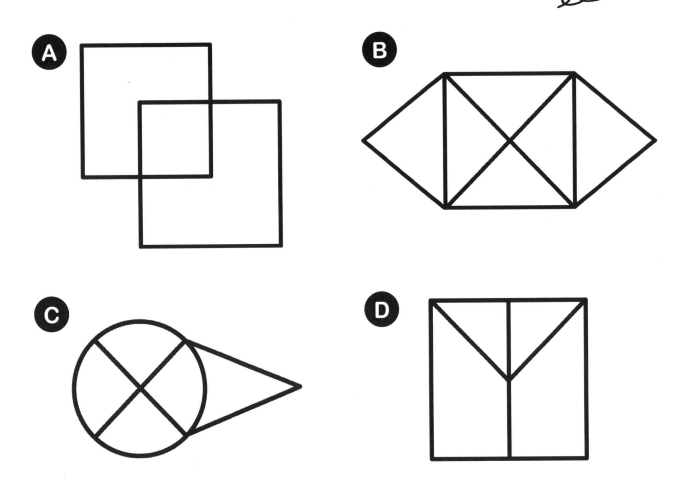

WORD CHAIN CHALLENGE

Changing one letter at a time, can you complete the word chain below from left to right. Check out the picture clues.

6 X 6 Sudoku

Put numbers in the empty squares so that every row, column, and every rectangle with thicker lines includes the numbers 1, 2, 3, 4, 5, and 6.

A

	3		6	5	
4			3		2
2		3	5		1
		1		4	3
	1	5	4		6
6	2			3	

B

5	3			2		4
6	2	4			1	
	5				2	1
1			2			5
				4	3	6
3			6	1		

C

			3	6	5
3		5	4		
	4		2		3
		3		4	6
6	2	1			4
5	3		6	1	

D

4				3		1
3			6	4	5	
	2		5			3
			3	6		5
	6				3	4
5	3			2	1	

33

FILL THE GAPS

Study the five dessert sequences from left to right and fill the gaps.

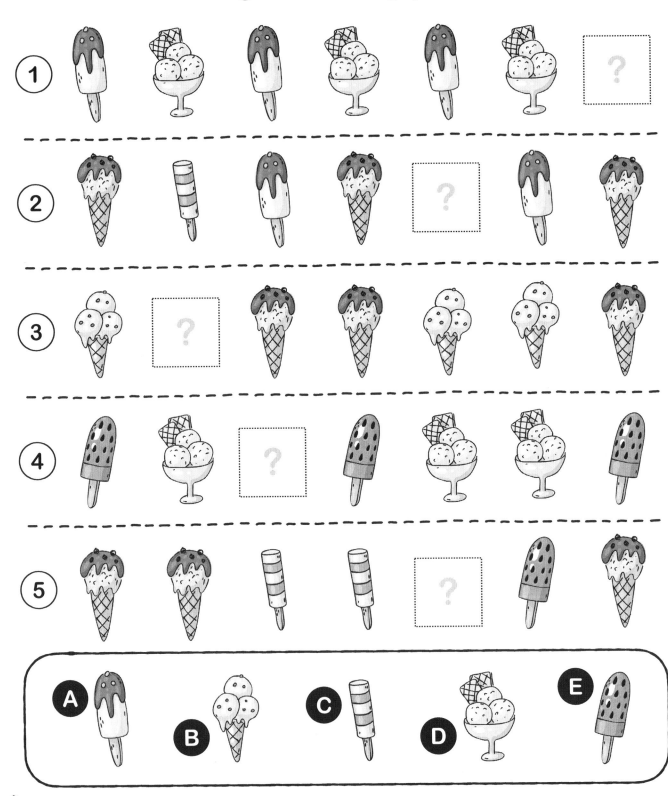

WORD CIRCLE

This circle of letters can help you solve the crossword puzzle below. All the answers can be spelled out using the letters from the circle. However, you can't use a letter more than once in a word.

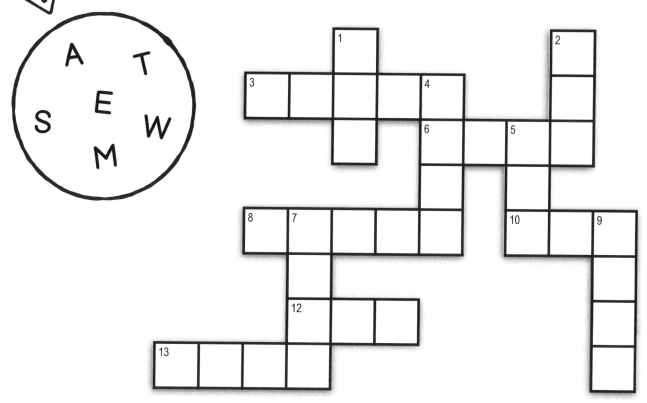

DOWN

1 A type of hot drink

2 What you do when you're hungry

4 The flesh of an animal

5 A tool for cutting wood

7 The opposite of east

9 A group of players who compete as one side in a game or sport

ACROSS

3 The hot gas produced when water boils

6 The opposite of west

8 The liquid on our skin when it's hot

10 Not dry

12 Home to dolphins and whales

13 A thing that you can sit on

TWO OF A KIND

Help the confused dog to find 6 pairs of identical faces!

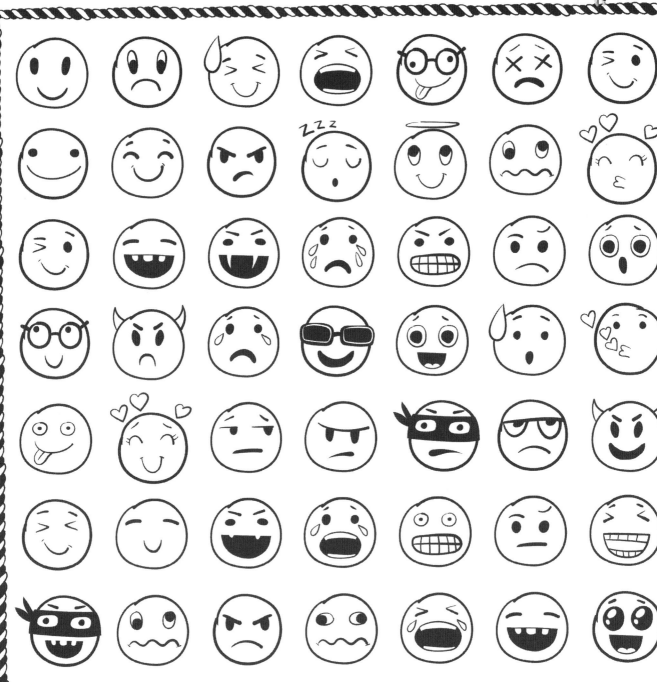

DRAW IT!

Follow these step-by-step instructions to learn to draw these cool vehicles!

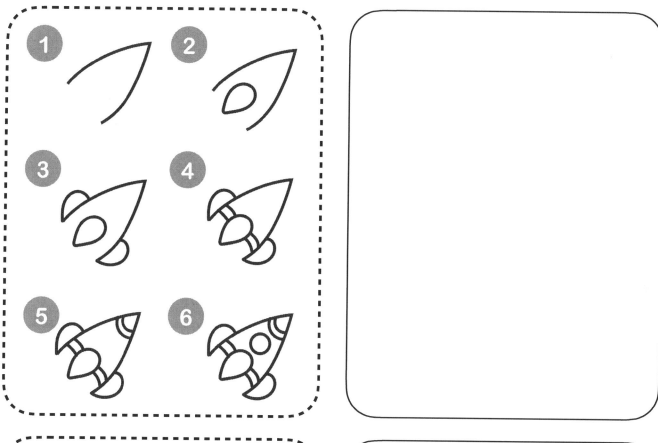

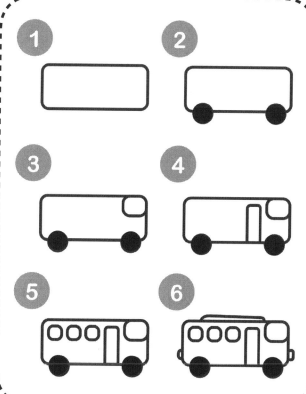

WHICH MYTHICAL CREATURE ARE YOU?

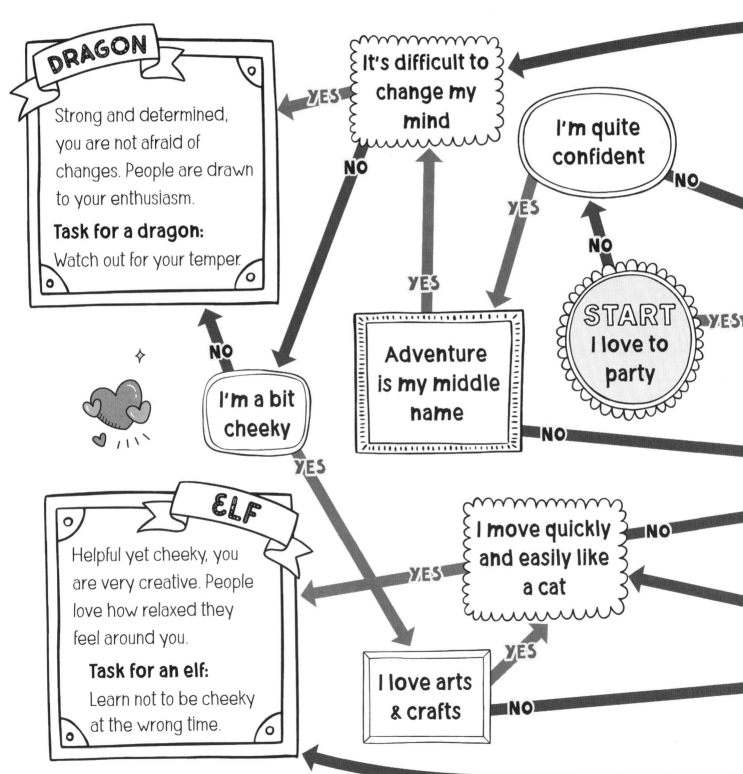

Answer the questions to reveal which creature you are in the mythical world! Do the test a few times as you might be a combination of a few creatures...

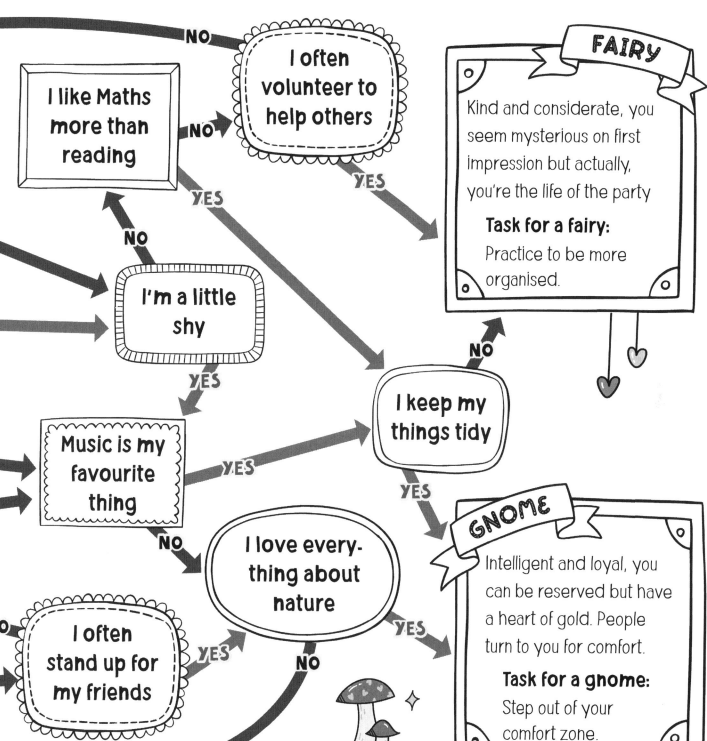

ANIMAL SOUNDS WORD SEARCH

Can you find these words in the grid below?

MOO	BLEAT	BELLOW	CLUCK
SQUEAK	GRUNT	CHEEP	HOOT
SHRIEK	PURR	BUZZ	GROWL

```
W E T E A F L W O R G C W O H
R M C D A J B X P G K L J O H
O G R U N T Z E W E W B I M A
V Y J P I M V Q L I I R T P S
H B W R N D S T W L N V U R G
N E R Y T D H M T O O H V U I
Q U J E I X R X D U F W W C W
P D S T V D I D O P H C H Z R
F E B T F O E A S J I E X E O
Z W U L P R K K D V E A U Z B
C M Z Q J T F U X P T O O X Q
H L Z W Z G A Z N E L H H X D
C L U I Q E K E Y S Q U E A K
X K T C W J B E L H J F L W O
Z K U M K L E S P B F L C Z I
```

SPELL IT OUT

Write down the first letter of each picture to reveal another animal sound.

 _   _   _   _   _

DOMINOES

Place these domino pieces in the grey spaces below to complete the domino chain.

Each domino has two halves, only the halves with the same number can touch each other. For example, this domino has six dots on one half and zero dots on the other, so only dominoes with six dots or zero dots can be placed next to it.

SPOT THE DIFFERENCE

Find the 10 differences between these two pictures.

TREASURE HUNT!

Work out the missing letters in the word puzzles below and cross out the corresponding row or column on the map. The map square left open is where the treasure is hidden!

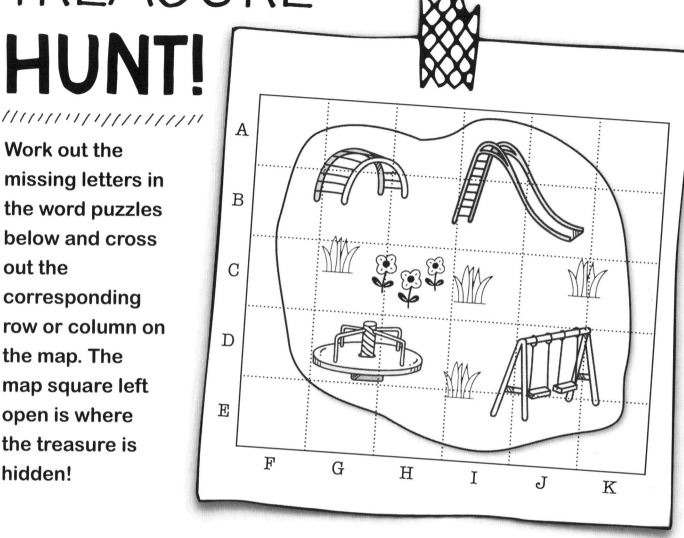

M_P

MON_EY

DU_K

_LOW_R

_OG

SWIN_

BENC_

EMO_I

I SPY

Can you find all these different vehicles and count how many of each there are?

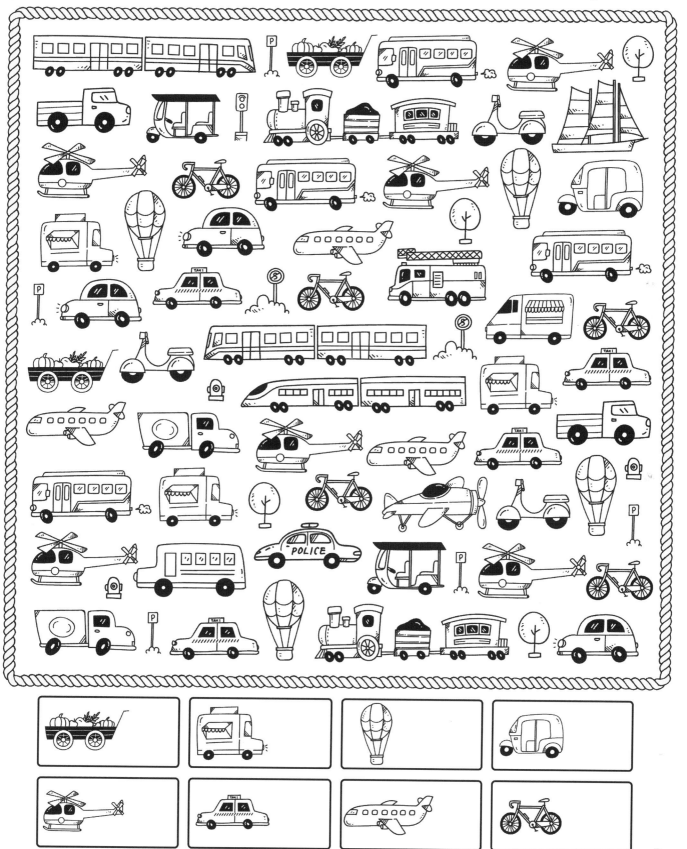

NUMBER PYRAMID

In this pyramid, the number in each square is the sum of the two numbers below it. Can you fill in all the empty squares?

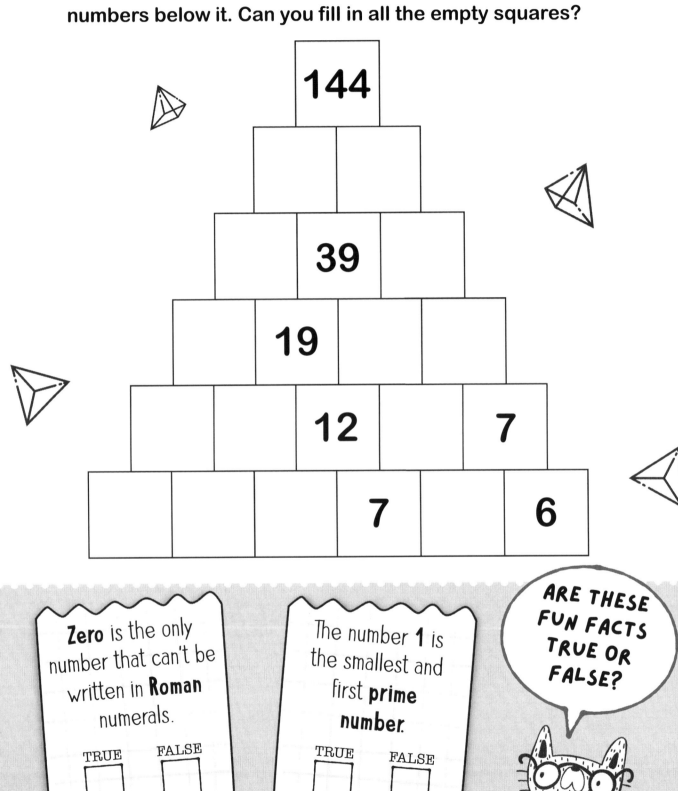

Zero is the only number that can't be written in **Roman** numerals.

TRUE ☐   FALSE ☐

The number **1** is the smallest and first **prime number**.

TRUE ☐   FALSE ☐

ARE THESE FUN FACTS TRUE OR FALSE?

46

NEIGHBOUR PUZZLE

The four children below are neighbours. Following the clues they give, can you figure out who lives in which house?

6 X 6 Sudoku

Put numbers in the empty squares so that every row, column, and every box with thicker lines includes the numbers 1, 2, 3, 4, 5, and 6.

A

6	2	3		1	
1			6		3
2	4		1		
		1		4	6
	6	2		5	1
	1		3	6	

B

3	1	5	6		
	2	6			1
2		1		6	4
	5		1		3
5	4			1	
		2	4	3	

C

5		2		6	3
	4	3			2
	6		5	2	
4		5		1	
	5	4	6		1
1			2		5

D

		1	2	4	
4		6	5		
	1	3	4		2
6	4				3
2	6		3	1	
1				2	4

48

SEASONAL JUMBLES

Look at these jumbled pictures, each of them contains 5 different things. Can you spot what they are?

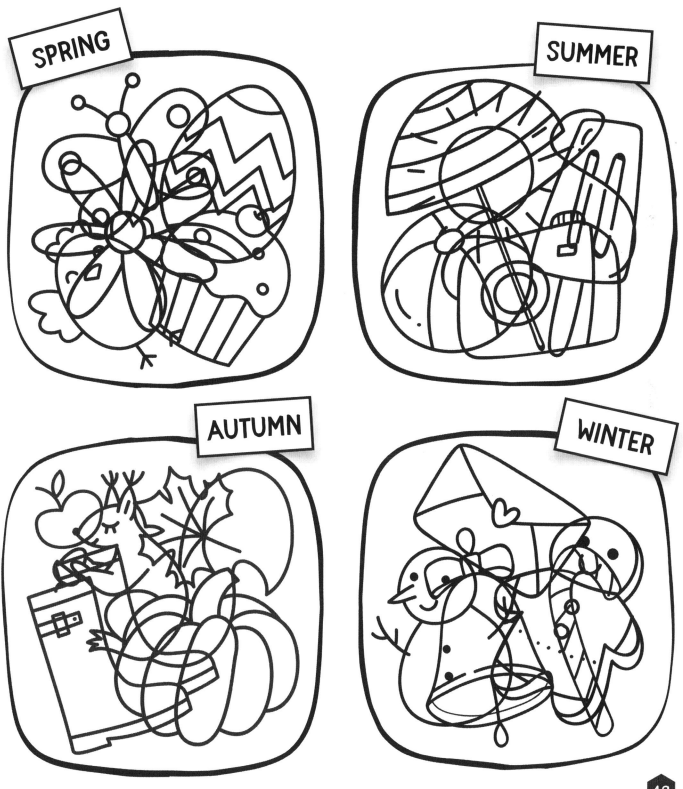

COLOUR IN THIS POSTER

You don't Have To Be PERFECT To Be Amazing

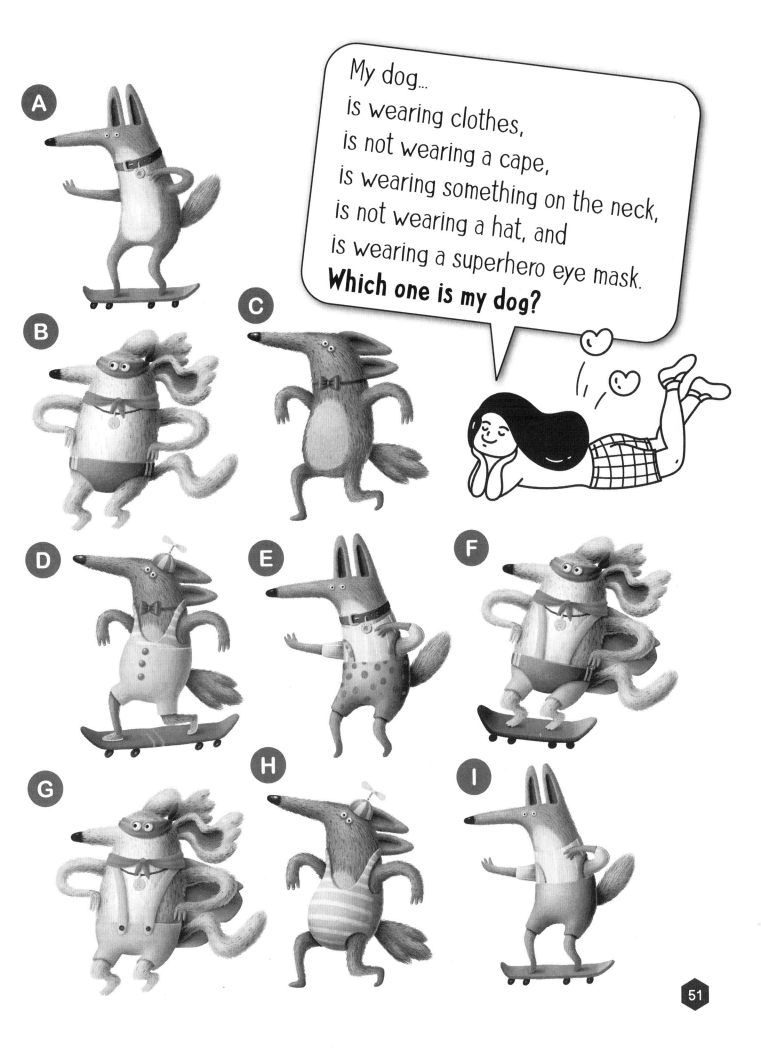

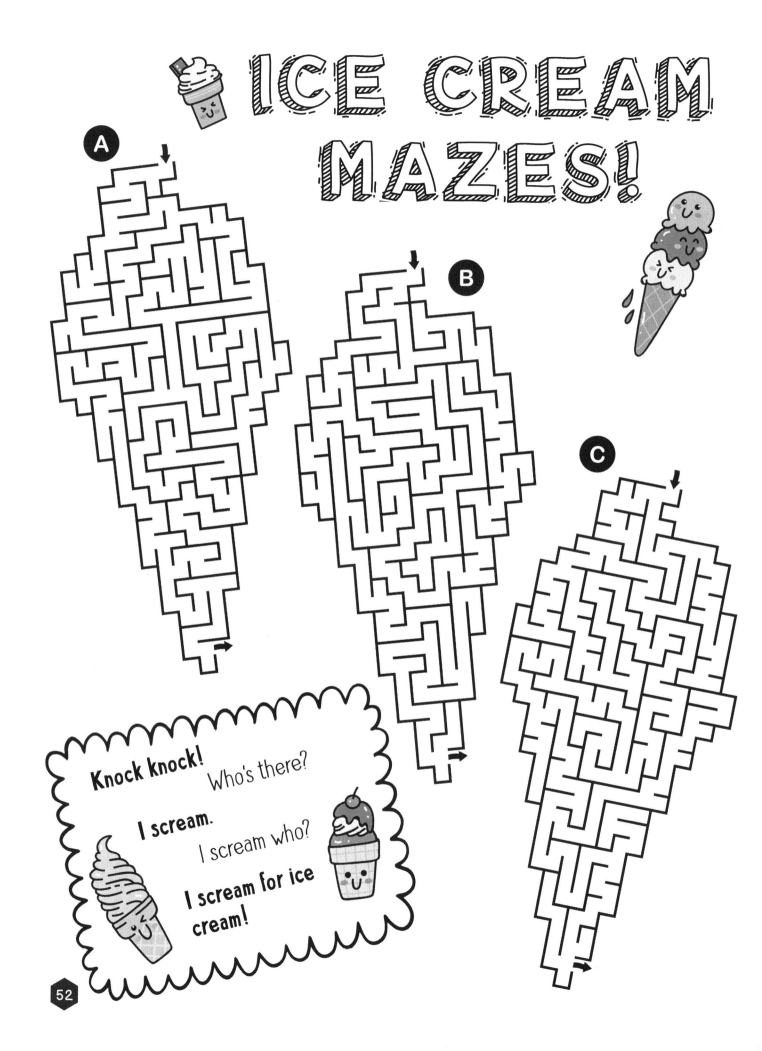

ARROW WORDS

The clues of this puzzle are in the grey squares, and the arrow from the clue points where the answer word should go. All the words go from left to right, or top to bottom, no matter which direction the arrow points. Some of the clues are pictures!

What ballerinas do ▶					
2 is an even ___			Halloween trick ___ treat ◀		Relax for a while. Take a ___ ▼
⌐					
🧱		💪 / ♠ ▶			
⌐					
Twice as much ⌐		Opposite of front ⌐		▲ ✓	

WORD JIGSAW

Do you believe in magic? Solve this word jigsaw to find out what the famous author Roald Dahl wrote about magic.

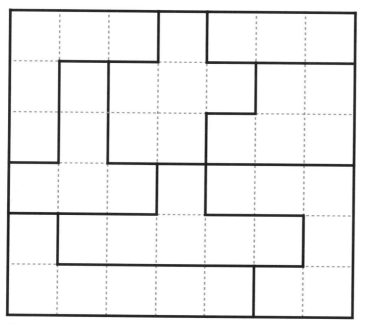

Write the letters from the jigsaw pieces into the correct squares, then read the answer.

WRITE IT DOWN HERE

ODD ONE OUT!

Spot **3** odd things in each of the two pictures!

You can hold me in your left hand but not your right. What am I?   A

I belong to you, but other people use me more than you do. What am I?   B

I'm light as a feather, yet the strongest person in the world can't hold me for five minutes. What am I?   C

If you're running in a race and you just pass the person in second place, what place are you in?   D

HERE ARE SOME RIDDLES FOR YOU!

I have many keys but I can't open a single lock. What am I?   E

I'm tall when I'm young, and I'm short when I'm old. What am I?   F

NUMBER CHALLENGE

Can you fit all these numbers into the grid below? Some numbers have been revealed to help you get started.

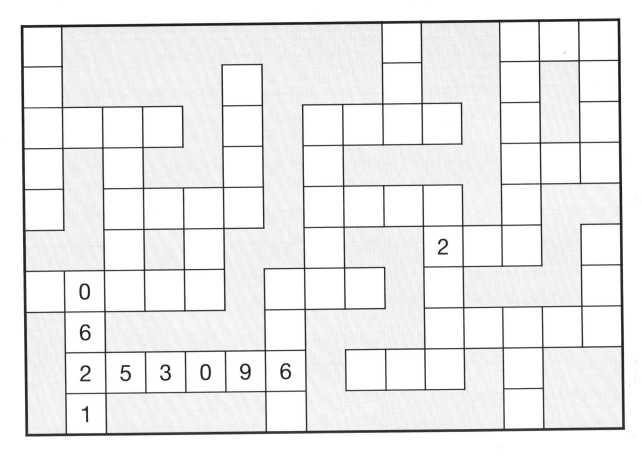

3 DIGITS
241 684
359 821
406 781
435 921
645

4 DIGITS
~~0621~~ 4085
1525 4259
3005 8591
3361 8853

5 DIGITS
10391
35964
32136
43815
64899
95413

6 DIGITS
~~253096~~
773631

OPPOSITE CROSSWORD

Are you ready for a brain exercise? All the clues for this crossword puzzle are the opposite of the answers.

DOWN

2 Outside
4 Early
5 Easy
7 Dark
8 After
9 Dry
10 Sad
14 Tall

ACROSS

1 Narrow
3 Hot
6 Left
11 Cheap
12 Bottom
13 Bad
15 Deep
16 Full

DOT TO DOT

Join the dots to uncover what is in the clouds.

AIRCRAFT SPELLING

Can you unscramble these three flying vehicles?

A. PARIANEL
B. TEOKCR
C. HCLEIOETPR

BIRD WORD SEARCH

Find all these birds in the grid below.

PENGUIN   ROBIN   HAWK   SWAN
PUFFIN   PARROT   GOOSE   FLAMINGO
EAGLE   KIWI   TURTLEDOVE   SEAGULL
VULTURE   OSTRICH WOODPECKER   TURKEY

```
A X K U R K W T L L W N F E O M B P M M
P P F U J Y H Z W L H D L X D K T B L H
U A E D S P Y O P U F F I N L Z Y Z S C
T H Y N Q A L H G G M C L T T V Z V L I
S Y T M G C T G O A V D S S R H V H M R
V T J C L U J B H E P I X D W T X M J T
A E E L R F I X K S Y W L N I A Y Y D S
R T A K F D L N G P N E R O Z Y N A D O
E P E G L O C U Y Z R R E F X V K M A A
K Y O M L K L C B U Q R J W J W R N K T
C V P Y Z E I L T X G E H S X F H E U E
E K O H T O O L S A E V O D E L T R U T
P Q X S M H U H L Q J D E A I A F V K A
D A P V B V H D N E O Y S X S M H B J L
O Q R J K J H F W H S H T S Q I Z K F O
O L Y R G F Y O P A F O L X R N K Z Q D
W J R B O L O F H J N G O U Z G F I B T
J O Q D U T X Z A T U H W G X O N B W F
X G K B Z O D Q W K U N K Q A R M T D I
T J U H B J V S K V A N V G R O B I N G
```

60

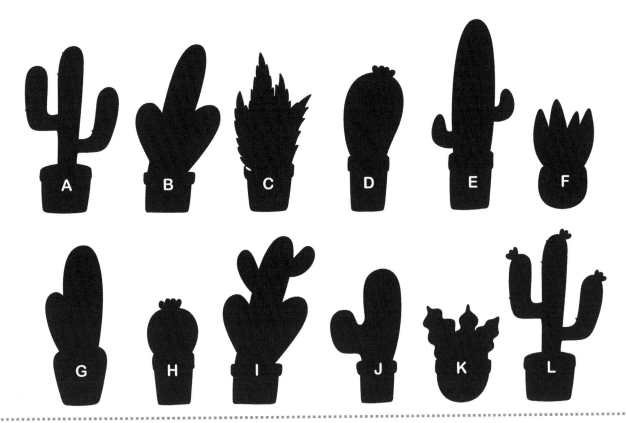

SHADOW MATCH

Can you pair each shadow with the appropriate cactus below?

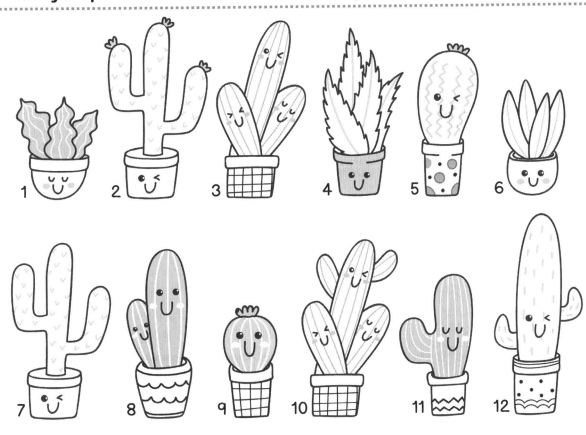

DRAW IT!

Follow these step-by-step instructions to learn to draw these cute animals!

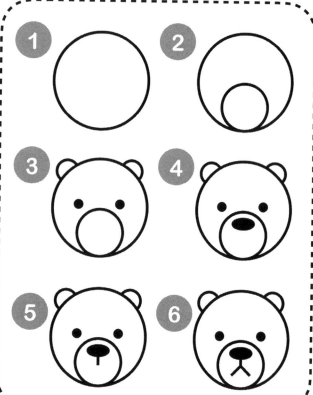

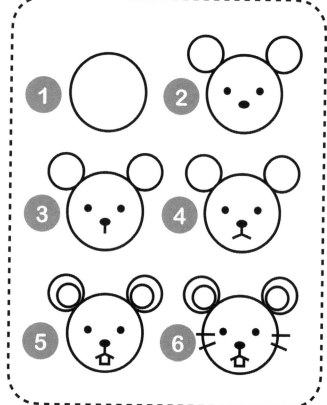

BROKEN WORDS

Can you read the clues below and piece these broken words back together? They are words for different types of vehicles.

CLUES

1. Vehicles on the railway
2. A cab
3. A cyclist's two-wheel vehicle
4. A large road vehicle for carrying goods
5. An emergency vehicle for sick or injured people
6. A farm vehicle
7. A vehicle with a kitchen and sleeping area
8. A vehicle that slides across ice or snow

TA, SLE, AIN, CK, YCLE, TR, TRA, XI, BIC, CAMP, ERVAN, CTOR, AMBU, TRU, DGE, LANCE

1. _ _ _ _ _
2. _ _ _ _
3. _ _ _ _ _ _ _
4. _ _ _ _ _
5. _ _ _ _ _ _ _ _ _
6. _ _ _ _ _ _ _
7. _ _ _ _ _ _ _
8. _ _ _ _ _ _

9 X 9 Sudoku

Put numbers in the empty squares so that every row, column, and every box with thicker lines includes the numbers 1, 2, 3, 4, 5, 6, 7, 8, and 9.

	2	3			7		8	5
5		8			9	7		2
				8		4	9	3
	9	5					4	
	3	1				9	5	7
			7			3		1
3					2	8		
6								
1			4	5	8		3	

JOKE TIME

What do you have if you hold 5 apples in one hand and 10 apples in another?

Very **big** hands!

TREASURE HUNT!

Read the pirate captain's description and find his treasure!

The island where I buried my treasure has a sandy beach on one side and a cliff on the other side.

When standing on the beach you can see some other islands.

There is a hut on the island, and I buried the treasure underneath a palm tree near a river.

Which one is my island?

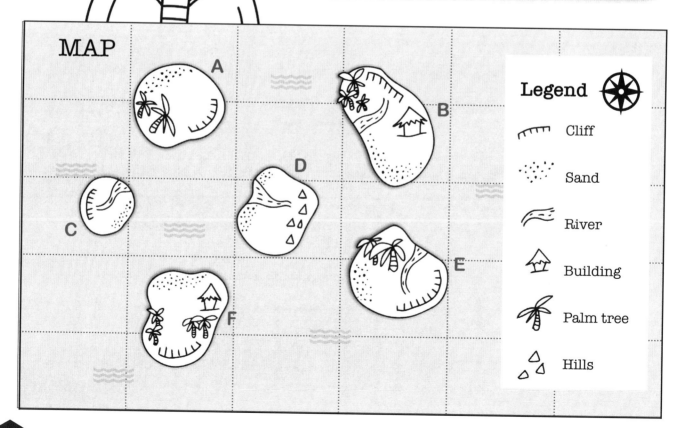

WOULD YOU RATHER?

Talk with your friends or family to find out each other's choices. Do they choose the same as you?

Would You Rather
be incredible at drawing
or
a fantastic musician?

Would You Rather
kiss a frog
or
meet a scary dragon?

Would You Rather
be as small as an ant
or
as big as an elephant?

Would You Rather
have roast chicken for breakfast
or
cereal for dinner?

Would You Rather
visit the Moon
or
the centre of the Earth?

Would You Rather
never have ice cream
or
never have cake?

ARROW WORDS

The clues of this puzzle are in the grey squares, and the arrows from the clue point to the squares where the answer words should go. All the words go from left to right, or top to bottom, no matter which direction the arrow points. Some clues are pictures!

SHADOW WORD GUESS

Observe the shadows below and write down the words in the grid. You'll find the answer to what has this boy found on the beach in the gray column.

The boy has found a

_ _ _ _ _ _ _ _

SPOT THE DIFFERENCE
Find the 10 differences between these two pictures.

NUMBER CHALLENGE

Can you fit all these numbers into the grid below? One of the numbers has been revealed to help you get started.

3 DIGITS	4 DIGITS		5 DIGITS		6 DIGITS
043	0750	3125	18807	50367	~~634382~~
609	1578	6150	32090	50503	804275
764	2791	8485	33735	55780	
798	2949	9401	41087	55842	
893	3109	9664	44174	77443	

COMIC TIME

Create your own comic story. Here are some ideas if you need inspiration...
- An adventure to a mysterious place
- Your version of a classic fairy tale
- An encounter with your favourite movie character

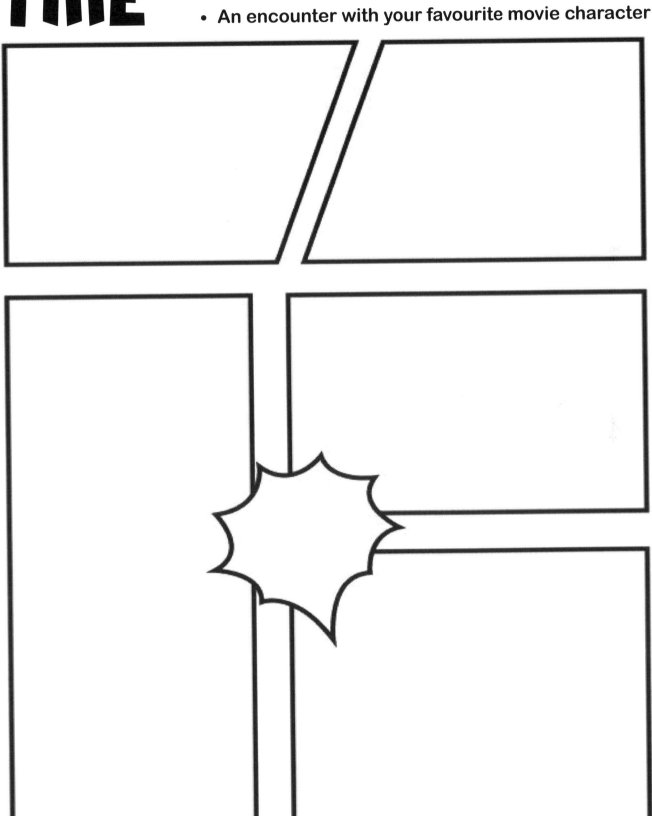

SPOT THE ODD CATS!

Two of the cats in the picture are not doing the same yoga pose as another one. Can you spot them?

MINI PUZZLE

Match the shapes to make five circles!

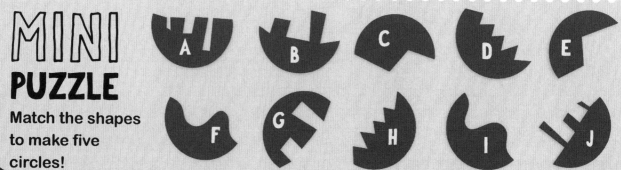

DOMINO CHALLENGE

Arrange the dominoes below to fit into the grid. The number of dots on the domino must match the number in the grid, and the dominoes must not overlap with each other. The first couple of them are revealed to help you get started.

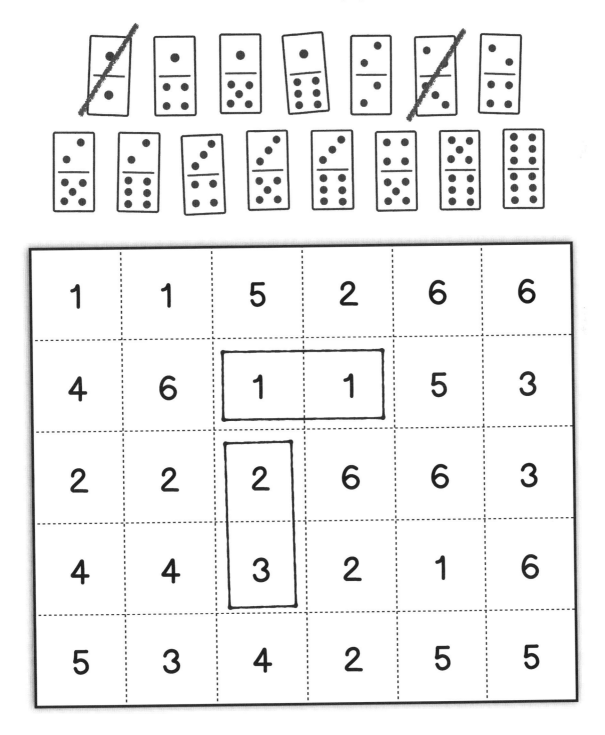

COLOUR BY NUMBERS

1 - LIGHT BLUE 4 - YELLOW
2 - DARK BLUE 5 - WHITE
3 - ORANGE

MISSING NUMBERS

The stacks of blocks below are missing some numbers. Can you add numbers 1, 2, 3, 4, or 5 in the empty blocks so that every row and every column contain all five numbers?

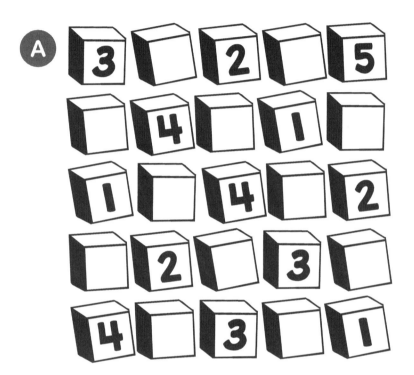

9 X 9 Sudoku

Put numbers in the empty squares so that every row, column, and every box with thicker lines includes the numbers 1, 2, 3, 4, 5, 6, 7, 8, and 9.

	4	2			3		6	
7		9			8	3	4	1
6		8				5		
3	9				4		8	
2		6						3
5					2	1		
	6	3	2		7		5	4
	7			8		6	3	
			9			7		

WHAT'S DIFFERENT?

Each of the unicorns has one thing different from the first one. Can you spot each of the differences?

I SPY

Can you find all these different Christmas items and count how many of each there are?

MOON WORD SEARCH

Can you find all of these words in the circle below?

- CRATERS
- DUST
- NIGHT
- CRESCENT
- FULL MOON
- NEW MOON
- QUARTER
- ORBIT
- ECLIPSE
- PHASES
- TIDES
- LUNAR
- STAR
- MONTH
- MOONLIGHT
- SATELLITE
- ASTRONAUT
- APOLLO
- SKY
- RISING

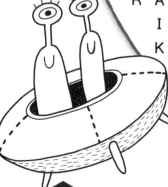

DOT TO DOT

Join the dots to reveal the vehicle!

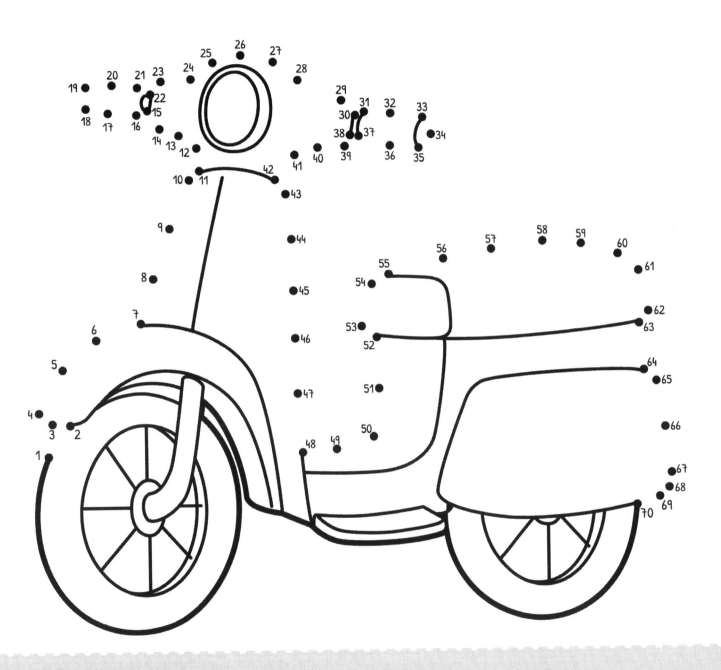

JOKE TIME

Why did the **spider** buy a **car**?

He wants to go for a **spin**!

FRUIT LOGIC!

Study each of the sequences from left to right, can you tell what the next two fruits should be?

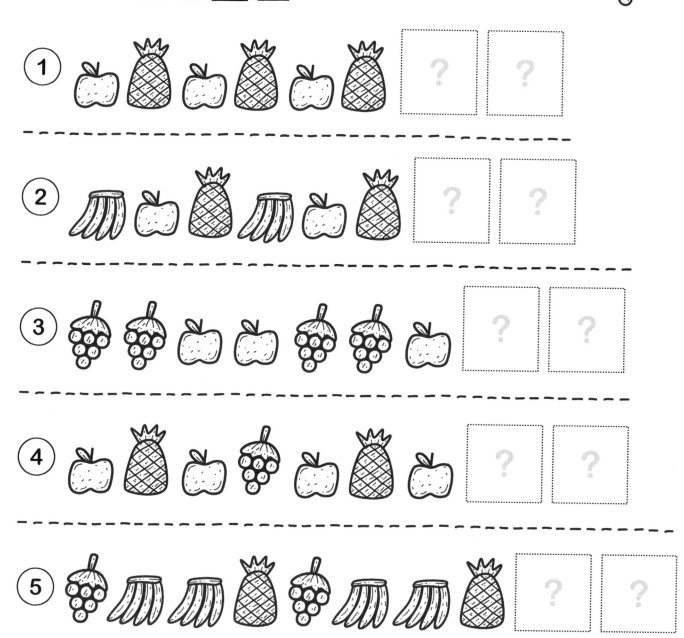

TRICKY JOKES
Can you find the punchline of these jokes?

1. What did the grizzly bears say when they saw campers in sleeping bags?
2. What does a cloud wear under its raincoat?
3. What do you call a dog magician?
4. Why did the kid cross the playground?
5. What goes around the world but stays in one corner?

A. To get to the other slide.
B. Burritos!
C. A stamp!
D. Thunderwear!
E. A labracadabrador!

WORD SNAKE

Can you find all the listed words in the grid? You can move up, down, or sideways but not diagonally.

- CLOWN
- ~~JOKE~~
- JESTER
- COMEDIAN
- FUNNY
- LAUGH
- COMEDY
- SLAPSTICK

C	O	M	E	D	E
S	C	L	O	Y	K
L	C	N	W	J	O
A	O	M	E	D	I
P	K	R	F	U	A
S	C	E	H	N	N
T	I	T	G	N	Y
J	E	S	U	A	L

83

DRESS THE DOGS

Give the dogs some colours and design more cool clothes for them!

WORD CIRCLE

This circle of letters can help you solve the crossword puzzle below. All the answers can be spelled out using the letters from the circle. However, you can't use a letter more than once in a word.

Letters in circle: H, T, A, E, D, S, R

DOWN

1. Part of our body above the neck
2. Colour of a fire engine
5. Organ that pumps blood
6. The planet we live on
8. Liquid from your eyes when crying
12. To give parts of food or toys to others

ACROSS

1. Not soft
3. long-eared rabbit-like animal with long, powerful hind legs
4. A thing to screen off light
7. Paintings and sculptures in galleries
9. Spend time with a book
10. Organ used for hearing
11. A thing you wear to cover your head

ANSWERS

PAGE 4

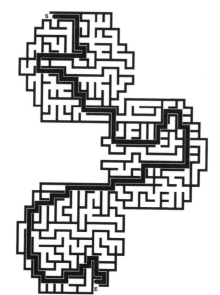

PAGE 5

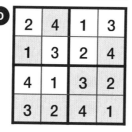

A
3	4	2	1
2	1	3	4
1	2	4	3
4	3	1	2

B
3	2	4	1
4	1	2	3
1	4	3	2
2	3	1	4

C
1	4	2	3
2	3	4	1
3	2	1	4
4	1	3	2

D
2	4	1	3
1	3	2	4
4	1	3	2
3	2	4	1

PAGE 6

PAGE 7

Picture C and F are exactly the same.

PAGE 9

PAGE 11

The dog's house is the one on the bottom left.

PAGE 13

PAGE 14

P	A	R	R	O	T
F	O	R	E	S	T
M	O	N	K	E	Y
B	A	N	A	N	A
A	M	A	Z	O	N
T	O	U	C	A	N

PAGE 15

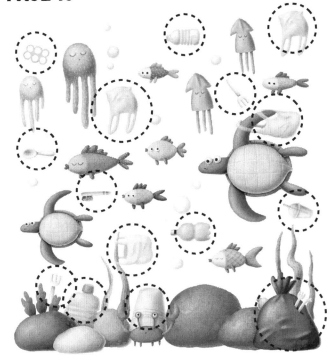

PAGE 16

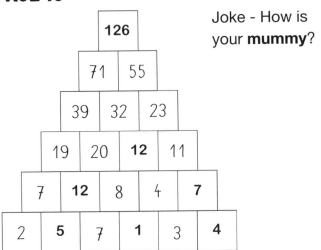

Joke - How is your **mummy**?

PAGE 17

1. fluffy
2. noisy
3. cheeky
4. naughty
5. clever
6. funny
7. cute
8. precious
9. sweet
10. beautiful

PAGE 18

A

1	2	4	3
4	3	1	2
3	1	2	4
2	4	3	1

B

1	3	2	4
2	4	1	3
3	1	4	2
4	2	3	1

C

1	3	2	4
4	2	3	1
3	4	1	2
2	1	4	3

D

4	2	1	3
1	3	4	2
2	1	3	4
3	4	2	1

PAGE 20

R	A	T					
E	L	E	P	H	A	N	T
D	R	A	G	O	N		

The national animal of Australia is the **red kangaroo.**

K	I	W	I					
A	N	T						
N	A	R	W	H	A	L		
G	I	R	A	F	F	E		
A	L	L	I	G	A	T	O	R
R	A	B	B	I	T			
O	W	L						
O	C	T	O	P	U	S		

PAGE 21

PAGE 23

N	U	K	U	L	E	L	E	F	B	A	N	J	O
A	C	C	O	R	D	I	O	N	G	T	E	V	F
Z	D	P	T	T	E	V	F	D	A	T	Y	M	W
N	I	L	O	I	V	B	X	M	X	N	V	K	Z
C	Y	F	T	V	A	Q	B	C	U	A	C	G	H
M	E	Y	F	B	T	O	M	F	L	U	T	E	A
J	H	N	U	I	U	R	R	G	O	K	N	G	O
G	S	T	O	R	S	Q	I	T	U	R	Q	E	Y
P	I	V	I	H	V	M	J	A	E	I	P	R	V
I	B	N	W	Q	P	M	U	D	N	F	T	G	Y
A	E	T	G	Z	N	O	R	R	H	G	X	A	R
N	Q	R	X	V	C	O	X	U	G	A	L	K	R
O	G	U	K	O	C	Z	E	A	F	Q	R	E	L
M	A	M	F	E	X	K	T	U	S	B	V	P	O
H	M	P	R	A	Z	W	O	N	T	D	N	O	L
K	B	E	C	U	U	A	Y	D	Z	M	P	H	L
U	Y	T	C	Z	D	R	U	M	Q	V	P	C	E
O	X	J	T	P	U	S	D	Y	M	A	Z	Q	C

PAGE 24

	T		H	O	T
R	E	C	I	P	E
	E		P	E	N
S	P	Y		N	
	E		N		M
M	E	L	O	D	Y

PAGE 25

PAGE 26

A - Shadow 6
B - Shadow 3

PAGE 30

LINE - **DINE** - **DIVE** - **FIVE** - GIVE

PAGE 31

PAGE 33

A
1	3	2	6	5	4
4	5	6	3	1	2
2	4	3	5	6	1
5	6	1	2	4	3
3	1	5	4	2	6
6	2	4	1	3	5

B
5	3	1	2	6	4
6	2	4	5	1	3
4	5	3	6	2	1
1	6	2	3	4	5
2	1	5	4	3	6
3	4	6	1	5	2

C
4	1	2	3	6	5
3	6	5	4	2	1
1	4	6	2	5	3
2	5	3	1	4	6
6	2	1	5	3	4
5	3	4	6	1	2

D
4	5	2	3	6	1
3	1	6	4	5	2
6	2	5	1	4	3
1	4	3	6	2	5
2	6	1	5	3	4
5	3	4	2	1	6

PAGE 34

1. A   2. C   3. B   4. D   5. E

PAGE 35

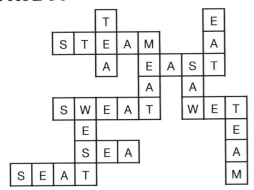

PAGE 36

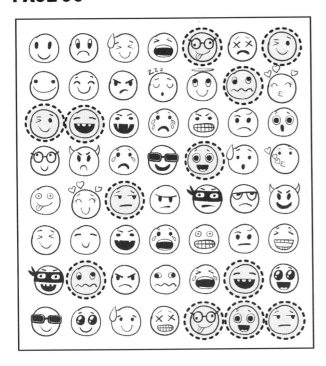

PAGE 40

Spell it out - **NEIGH**

PAGE 41

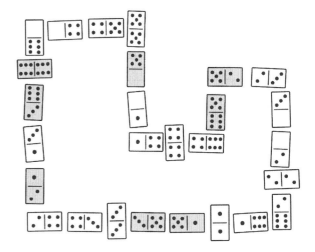

PAGE 42

PAGE 43

The treasure is hidden underneath the slide, in the map square of B and I.

PAGE 45

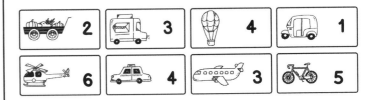

PAGE 46

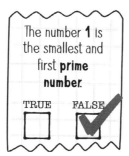

PAGE 47

C B A D

PAGE 48

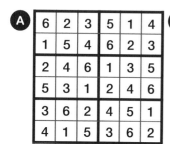
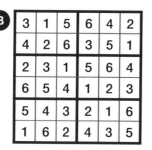
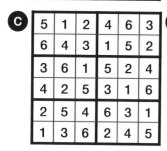
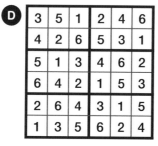

PAGE 49

- Spring - butterfly, Easter egg, flower, chick, cupcake
- Summer - umbrella, sun, ball, camera, ice lolly
- Autumn - apple, leaf, squirrel, welly boots, pumpkin
- Winter - snowman, Christmas card/envelope, candy cane, bell, gingerbread man

PAGE 51

B

PAGE 52

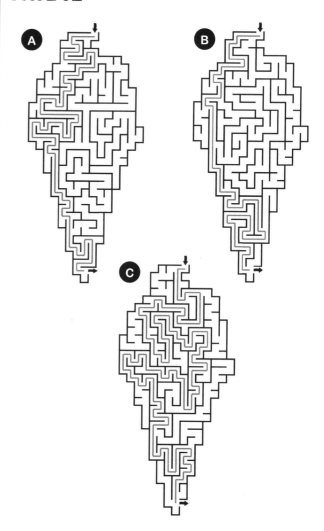

PAGE 53

	D	A	N	C	E
	O	R		H	
N	U	M	B	E	R
	B		A	C	E
B	L	O	C	K	S
	E		K		T

PAGE 54

T	H	O	S	E	W	H
O	D	O	N	'	T	B
E	L	I	E	V	E	I
N	M	A	G	I	C	W
I	L	L	N	E	V	E
R	F	I	N	D	I	T

"Those who don't believe in magic will never find it."

PAGE 55

PAGE 56

A. Your right elbow
B. Your name
C. Your breath
D. Second place
E. A piano
F. A candle

PAGE 57

6									4			7	8	1
4					3				3			7		5
8	5	9	1		0		4	2	5	9		3		2
9		5			0		3					6	4	5
9		4	0	8	5		8	8	5	3		3		
		1		2			1			2	4	1		6
1	0	3	9	1		3	5	9		1				8
	6					3				3	5	9	6	4
	2	5	3	0	9	6		4	6	6		2		
	1					1						1		

PAGE 58

				W	I	D	E		C	O	L	D
					N			D			A	
					S		R	I	G	H	T	
					I			F			E	
B		B			D			F		W		H
R		E	X	P	E	N	S	I	V	E		A
I		F						C		T	O	P
G	O	O	D		S			U				P
H		R		S	H	A	L	L	O	W		Y
T		E			O			T				
					R							
		E	M	P	T	Y						

PAGE 59

A. AIRPLANE
B. ROCKET
C. HELICOPTER

PAGE 60

PAGE 61

A. 7 G. 8
B. 3 H. 9
C. 4 I. 10
D. 5 J. 11
E. 12 K. 1
F. 6 L. 2

PAGE 63

1. Train
2. Taxi
3. Bicycle
4. Truck
5. Ambulance
6. Tractor
7. Campervan
8. Sledge

PAGE 64

9	2	3	6	4	7	1	8	5
5	4	8	3	1	9	7	6	2
7	1	6	2	8	5	4	9	3
2	7	9	5	3	1	6	4	8
4	3	1	8	2	6	9	5	7
8	6	5	7	9	4	3	2	1
3	5	4	1	6	2	8	7	9
6	8	2	9	7	3	5	1	4
1	9	7	4	5	8	2	3	6

PAGE 65

PAGE 66

Island B has the buried treasure.

PAGE 69

	S	P	O	T	S
	P	E		R	
J	I	G	S	A	W
	R		T	I	E
B	A	N	A	N	A
	L		R		K

PAGE 70

			S	U	N		
	K	I	T	E			
	C	R	A	B			
	A	I	R	P	L	A	N	E
			F	I	S	H	
J	E	L	L	Y	F	I	S	H
S	U	N	G	L	A	S	S	E	S
		S	E	A	H	O	R	S	E

The boy has found a **starfish**.

PAGE 71

PAGE 72

1	5	7	8		5	5	7	8	0		6		
	5					0				4	4	1	7	4
	8		6	3	4	3	8	2		3		5		1
	4		0			6		9				0		0
3	2	0	9	0		7	7	4	4	3				8
1				3				9		1	8	8	0	7
2	7	9	1		3		8			0			7	
5		6			7	6	4		7	9		8	5	
		6			3		8					9	4	0	1
8	0	4	2	7	5		5	0	5	0	3			

PAGE 74

- A + J
- B + G
- C + E
- D + H
- F + I

PAGE 75

1	1	5	2	6	6
4	6	1	1	5	3
2	2	2	6	6	3
4	4	3	2	1	6
5	3	4	2	5	5

PAGE 77

A)
3 1 2 4 5
2 4 5 1 3
1 3 4 5 2
5 2 1 3 4
4 5 3 2 1

B)
5 3 1 4 2
2 4 5 3 1
1 2 3 5 4
3 1 4 2 5
4 5 2 1 3

PAGE 78

1	4	2	5	9	3	8	6	7
7	5	9	6	2	8	3	4	1
6	3	8	7	4	1	5	2	9
3	9	7	1	6	4	2	8	5
2	1	6	8	5	9	4	7	3
5	8	4	3	7	2	1	9	6
8	6	3	2	1	7	9	5	4
9	7	1	4	8	5	6	3	2
4	2	5	9	3	6	7	1	8

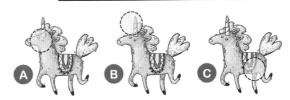

PAGE 79

PAGE 80

PAGE 82

1. DB 2. AD 3. DC 4. CD 5. CA

PAGE 83

1. B
2. D
3. E
4. A
5. C

PAGE 85

			H	A	R	D			
	H	A	R	E		E			
			A			A			
			D			D			
	S	H	A	D	E				
			E		A	R	T		
R	E	A	D		R		R	E	A	R
			R		T		A		
H	A	T		S	H	A	R	E	

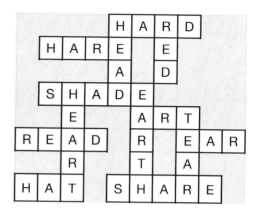

© **Copyright (2022) by Beaky and Starlight Ltd - All rights reserved.**

This document is geared towards providing exact and reliable information in regards to the topic and issue covered. The publication is sold with the idea that the publisher is not required to render accounting, officially permitted, or otherwise, qualified services. If advice is necessary, legal or professional, a practiced individual in the profession should be ordered.

In no way is it legal to reproduce, duplicate, or transmit any part of this document in either electronic means or in printed format. Recording of this publication is strictly prohibited and any storage of this document is not allowed unless with written permission from the publisher. All rights reserved.

The information provided herein is stated to be truthful and consistent, in that any liability, in terms of inattention or otherwise, by any usage or abuse of any policies, processes, or directions contained within is the solitary and utter responsibility of the recipient reader. Under no circumstances will any legal responsibility or blame be held against the publisher for any reparation, damages, or monetary loss due to the information herein, either directly or indirectly.

Respective authors own all copyrights not held by the publisher.

The information herein is offered for informational purposes solely, and is universal as so. The presentation of the information is without contract or any type of guarantee assurance.

The trademarks that are used are without any consent, and the publication of the trademark is without permission or backing by the trademark owner. All trademarks and brands within this book are for clarifying purposes only and are the owned by the owners themselves, not affiliated with this document.

Produced by Beaky and Starlight Ltd.

Published : June 2022

ISBN:9798837831515

For more information about the publisher, please visit:

www.facebook.com/BeakyAndStarlight/

ALSO AVAILABLE IN AMAZON:

ISBN 979-8561671821

ISBN 979-8754213760

ISBN 979-8557614337

ISBN 979-8569221776

ISBN 979-8575928928

ISBN 979-8772690147

ISBN 979-8771423029